YOU NEED A

MANIFESTO

T0384479

YOU NEED A
MANIFESTO

How to Craft Your Convictions and Put Them to Work

Charlotte Burgess-Auburn
Manifestos and art by Rick Griffith
Illustrations by Annie Marino

TEN SPEED PRESS
California | New York

HASSO PLATTNER
Institute of Design at Stanford

CONTENTS

4 CURATE

5 CULTIVATE

MANIFESTOS BY RICK GRIFFITH

1 MANIFESTO FOR THE STARTERS: HOW TO BEGIN AND BEGIN AND START 2 SO YOU ARE READY TO MAKE A
REVOLUTION: EVERYTHING THAT HAPPENS HERE IS PLURAL 3 A MANIFESTO IN TIME: EVERYONE (THING) IN
ITS RIGHT (TIME AND) PLACE 4 A MANIFESTO OF MANIFESTOS: COLLECT THEM ALL
5 NEVER GO ALONE: IT FEELS BETTER TOGETHER

THINGS HAVE CHANGED, PEOPLE

— BOB DYLAN

A Note from the d.school

At the Stanford d.school, design is a verb. It's an attitude to embody and a way to work. The core of that work is trying, to the best of one's abilities, to help things run more smoothly, delight more people, and ease more suffering. This holds true for you, too—whether design is your profession or simply a mindset you bring to life.

Founded in 2005 as a home for wayward thinkers, the d.school was a place where independent-minded people could gather, try out ideas, and make change. A lot has shifted in the decade or so since, but that original exuberant and resourceful attitude is as present today as it was then.

Our series of ten guides is here to offer you the same inventiveness, insight, optimism, and perseverance that we champion at the d.school. Like a good tour guide, these handbooks will help you find your way through unknown territory and introduce you to some fundamental ideas that we hope will become cornerstones in your creative foundation.

Learn how to craft with curiosity and build new ideas with *This Is a Prototype*. Find your *Creative Hustle* and put your talents to work in the world. And now, get ready to write your own script and work with purpose.

You Need a Manifesto!

love,
   the d.school

There's No Time Like the Present

Is it just me? Or do you feel like this moment, right now, is the most complex, fraught, pivotal, dangerous, and important moment that has ever been? Change is upon us. The future is (mercifully) unwritten, but increasingly unknown. Never mind the answers; we don't even have the questions that will arise. It's an awkward situation at best, and terrifying at worst. It feels like history is hurtling toward us like the dinosaur-killing asteroid, and we're still trying to get to work on time.

Many arcs are playing out that will require all our power to bend them toward the justice we know is there. And, yes, it rests on your shoulders to do the work. Right now, with the tools in your hands, creative work is more powerful than ever. Anything that can be imagined can be made. Your work will move mountains, cure plagues, sway rulers, and change the world. For good. And for ill.

You are responsible for your own learning, your own path, your own success, your own ethics. It's not easy to do both well and good. You need agency to act and humility to learn. To thrive in the tumultuous present and make some headway toward the future you're looking for, you'll have to get comfortable with managing a flood of choices, holding fast against the continuous threat of attention-drain, and doing daily battle with embedded and entrenched systems.

What do you believe in? What are you really after? How do you make sure the answers to these questions show up in your work?

You need tools to navigate the sea of change. You need the advice of a teacher, the encouragement of a friend, the hard-won knowledge of your own experience, the wisdom of a guru, the challenge of a goal. Some compass to carry with you on the crowded path of living. **You need a manifesto**, to recruit yourself into exercising your power as a creator and change maker. To filter the signal from the noise. To know—not just what you *can* do, but what you *should* do, what you *must* do, and *how* to do it.

What makes the tuning fork of your soul tremble with recognition? What resonates? What rings true? Seize it. Save it. Test it. Work it. When you are right, celebrate your victory. When you are wrong, change your assumptions.

You can write it in tiny print on a laminated card and keep it in your wallet. You can wheat paste it onto public buildings. You can tattoo it on your body. You can print it on T-shirts. You can write it as prose, poem, or song. You can borrow the words or breathe out your own. But have one. **Start one. Right now.**

STOP

TAKE A DEEP AND MEANINGFUL BREATH

SAY WHO YOU ARE
SAY WHERE YOU COME FROM
SAY WHERE YOU ARE GOING
SAY HOW YOU'll GET THERE
READ WHAT YOU'VE SAID

ERASE NOTHING

CAPTURE YOUR MOST

RELENTLESS THOUGHTS

EDIT NOTHING!

TAKE A DEEP AND MEANINGFUL BREATH

AND BE THAT PERSON

AND GO THERE.

REPEAT AS NECESSARY.

COMMENCE

Be Your Own Monk

A few years ago I went to a conference in Oxford, England. It was a cold, rainy, and raw April, not unusual for England but romantic in a way, with early morning mists hovering over the canals that thread in and around the city. The gardens seemed to burst out from behind the giant gates of ancient university courtyards and soaring stone buildings. A few days in, Debra, a colleague of mine from Stanford, also arrived. She was deeply involved in the content of this conference and in high demand from presenters and the attendees alike, meeting tables of people in the hotel dining room at 7:00 a.m. for breakfast, having one-on-ones over tea and coffee, and squeezing in appointments between presentations nearly all day long.

One morning, later in the week, I came down to breakfast fairly early and found Debra sitting in a chair in the hallway between the lobby and the dining room, crying. I gave her a hug (my instinctive reaction to pretty much every emotion) and found out that while she was here on one side of the world, back in California her beloved dog was dying. Her dog was being lovingly cared for by her husband, but Debra was faced with a moment of deep pain and a decision. All she really wanted to do was get on a plane and go home. But she also knew that by the time she arrived it might already be too late to say goodbye. And at the conference were people who needed her. She and they had invested time, energy, and many resources into creating this powerful moment for connecting around sustainable solutions to much bigger problems than the one she faced now. And yet the pain of her loss was palpable, and the decision was not an easy one to face.

Did I mention that Debra is Buddhist? She is. I had noticed earlier in the week that there was a Buddhist monk at the conference. His bright saffron robes and shaved head were hard to miss in the cold, gray English weather.

"Would you like me to find him?" I asked. "Perhaps he would have something to say that could help?"

"Thank you," she said, "but no. I already know what he will tell me." She stood up and gave me another hug. "I'm going to go walk along the canals for a while and be my own monk. I'll tell myself all the things I know I need to hear. And I'll see you later at the main presentation."

Let's all aspire to create a navigational practice as strong as Debra's. One that's so familiar that in honest moments of difficulty you can be your own monk—telling yourself what you already know you believe, making those tough decisions easier to make. "Be your own monk" is a part of my own manifesto now. My manifesto, like all the best kinds of navigational practices, doesn't tell me what's right or wrong in every instance. Rather, it makes clear to me what I believe, and I make the decisions.

This book will show you how to the use the tools of design to create your own manifesto. You'll learn how to identify your values and beliefs, articulate the behaviors that represent them, and craft them into a personal manifesto that you can use every day as a tool for making decisions and taking action.

A personal manifesto is the Swiss Army Knife of self-awareness. Your manifesto can give you the confidence to take risks that are important to you and be persistent about pursuing goals you actually care about. You can use it to synthesize new ideas and knowledge, react to change with coherence and consistency, inform your intuition, be authentic with others, and avoid situations that lead to regret. Your manifesto can be the life raft you build to keep your head above the waters of change, travel the oceans of new technology and complexity, and work your work a little wiser every day.

Recruit Yourself

In Latin, *manifesto* refers to an action "given with the hand (*manus*)," an encapsulation of belief intended to be public and passed from person to person. You might be familiar with political manifestos like *The Communist Manifesto* or religious manifestos known as creeds (*credo* means "I believe" in Latin). These are methods for the expression of personal beliefs, but also powerful tools for public recruitment to collective causes and political movements. In Europe, after the invention of movable type and the adoption of printing presses, many more people gained access to reading and writing as methods of learning and expression. The broadcast and development of new ideas, discoveries, and beliefs accelerated the development of individual rights and liberties through successive movements for social change. Manifestos were both a proclamation of new ideas and an invitation to participate as a part of those movements. People have continued to produce ideas and exchange them as manifestos as far and as fast as each new broadcast medium can take them.

Over time, with the addition of radio and television and the explosion of the internet, the landscape of publicly accessible ideas has become more and more crowded and anonymous, leaving many people feeling confused, jaded, and unmoored in a flood of manifesto-like content. Indeed, while the making of manifestos as a mechanism for self-expression has flourished, it has also been co-opted in destructive ways—into the service of corporate interests as advertising and marketing mumbo-jumbo. Far worse, manifestos have been used at times by repressive regimes as the hammer of propaganda or as a litmus test of legitimacy and a means of exclusion.

The time is right to redefine the manifesto as personal for the present moment. Manifestos have been a tool for recruiting people to collective causes—political, religious, artistic. But in this age, where it seems like everyone is being recruited by everyone else every moment of the day, you need a way to recruit yourself to your own cause, a method for collecting and considering your own power to create and to make positive change in a world that sorely needs it.

Creative work—the work of bringing ideas into the world, whatever kind they are—is hugely powerful. It is a particular kind of power: the power to generate, to make something where before there wasn't anything. The power to improve, to build on the work of others, and reach closer to an ideal. The power to influence, to engage people in new beliefs, activities, and behaviors. And the power to change it all. That is the impact of design.

Nearly every object and system you interact with every day has been designed. But that doesn't mean each has been designed well or even with good intentions. Designed work tinkers with our lives through our cultures, our tools, and our environments, but also our attention, our emotions, and our capacity to think and to communicate. Well-intended and poorly designed solutions can produce outcomes just as horrible as those of intentionally malicious ones. I am certain that Facebook did not intend to design a product that would weaken American democracy, but many side effects of the "social network" are seriously antisocial. Emerging technologies are just that—emergent—which means we often can't understand the full implications of what we are making. Making things better may have always been a part of creative work, but justice is a larger theme of this age. We are much more aware of how hard it is to design products and systems that produce fair outcomes for people across the globe and for the planet itself—and how easy it is to fail to account for the potential impact of our great new ideas.

The goals of equity and sustainability can produce more than enough work for all of us. But how can you find the right spot for your individual kind of creative work within a larger context of positive change, in a culture and environment that is constantly changing? To begin, you'll need to be able to envision goals worth pursuing and to cultivate some faith in your ability to achieve them without creating endless collateral damage. The world is as wide open as it ever was. To feel less unmoored, you need to create strong anchors to your values, develop ethical navigation tools, and describe honest destinations.

A modern manifesto is a statement of purpose and a script for action that will allow you, as a citizen of the creative world, to recruit yourself to your own cause, navigate bravely, and share your unique position with others.

What kind of personal guidance system do you need? *You, in particular.* What shorthand statement would stand in for your long thoughts or strong feelings? What sort of encouragement and advice would help you find your way? Perhaps you need a way to keep your voice steady in loud spaces or a way to test your mettle and keep you honest. You might require tactics to recognize and avoid empty promises, exclusion, and division. Your manifesto is less a map to the future than a compass for the present. And everyone's present is a different place. Whatever kind of guidance it is that you need, you should recognize it first and foremost as a living document that is built by, for, and about you.

Your personal manifesto can be one of liberation and self-identification, giving voice to individual ideas and beliefs while still participating in a collective culture. It should be applicable to you and your work in the moment, but capable of being questioned and revised before it becomes trite or dogmatic for you or for others. As you'll see later, when you create a manifesto with others, it's even more important to be mindful that it doesn't become so rigid that it serves as a test of acceptance—or so fluid that it is a useless exercise in lip service.

And while your personal manifesto doesn't have to be public to everyone, it does have to be public to you. You need to be able to work with it in the open, outside of your own head. A personal manifesto will help you identify your values, synthesize your learning, and articulate your best behaviors by externalizing ideas and feelings that are inside of you. By pulling your beliefs out of an interior, theoretical head space and placing them in the real world, you can see what you really think, critique your current behavior, and modify your goals. Most importantly, you can use your manifesto to make clear decisions and take action with intention.

Start Small

A personal manifesto can take many forms, but we're not talking about the errant musings of crackpot extremists here. You need some solid advice, inspiration, and support, preferably on the pithy side. There is a reason that most manifestos are short. Concise, powerful statements create a clear image in the mind's eye. They function as mental shortcuts to your goals, your values, and your ethics. They maintain access to these concepts that are more complicated and nuanced and allow you to conceptualize your choices, change your mindset, and reinforce the behaviors you want to have. Ultimately, they make it easier to act.

This is not about cat poster affirmations; it is about what is really happening in your work and life. We all need the opportunity to grow authentically, to develop a practice of self-awareness and improvement, to become aware of our weaknesses and biases, to cultivate our strengths and intuition. Your manifesto is a self-teaching feedback loop. It can be advice for moments of decision, a memory trigger to put you in the right stance for the work at hand, or a mantra of encouragement for moments when ambiguity or uncertainty has made you insecure.

SOME CONCISE

APHORISM
a concise statement of a principle

EXHORTATION
language intended to incite and encourage

PARABLE
a short story that teaches a moral or spiritual lesson

TRUISM
a true statement that is very commonly heard

MEME
a unit of cultural information spread by imitation

CREDO
a set of fundamental beliefs; a guiding principle

MOTTO
a short expression of a guiding principle

MAXIM
a general truth, fundamental principle, or rule of conduct

STATEMENTS,

IN A NUTSHELL

MANIFESTO
a written statement declaring publicly the intentions, motives, or views of its issuer

INVOCATION
the act or process of petitioning for help or support

EPIGRAM
a terse, sage, or witty and often paradoxical saying

MANTRA
a word or phrase that is repeated often or that expresses someone's basic beliefs

EVOCATION
the summoning of a spirit

ADVICE
recommendation regarding a decision or course of conduct

DECLARATION
the act of making known, or the document that makes known formally, officially, or explicitly

A MANIFESTO

WORK YOUR WORK.

It's easy to get lost in the middle of a complex project. A distillation of principles can create fixed points of reference in the ambiguous landscape of creative work. These mottos put you in the right mindset and help you know how to proceed in a stuck moment or anchor the phase of work you are in.

TRY ON NEW METHODS, IDENTITIES, OR BEHAVIORS.

The futurist Paul Saffo describes good projections as "strong opinions, lightly held." Strong statements, when treated as an intentional test, can help you to evaluate and evolve your beliefs by pushing boundaries and defining edges. Don't be afraid to shift and change as you move through your learning, your work, and your life.

TAKE RISKS THAT ARE IMPORTANT TO YOU.

You can lean on appeals to courage and fortitude to help you take risks that are important to you, push you out of your comfort zone, and persist in pursuing goals you actually care about.

IS TO...

MANAGE ADVERSITY AND HOLD YOUR GROUND.

Guiding principles can help you react to change and difficult situations with coherence and consistency. Acting in line with a broader set of ethics and values, even when it is difficult, can help you do the right thing and avoid situations that lead to regret.

COMMUNICATE YOUR IDENTITY, BE AUTHENTIC WITH OTHERS, CREATE TRUST.

Your manifesto can be a tool for connection. It begins with you, but it can spread to others, acting as a calling card for your unique position in the world, clearing the way for genuine connection, communication, and collaboration with others.

SYNTHESIZE YOUR LEARNING.

When you take in new ideas, they spend some time mingling with all the information and ideas you already know. As your new information interacts with all those ideas, you develop a sense of understanding that is uniquely yours. Sometimes a particular statement can capture that unique understanding and give you rapid access to it in the moments when you need it.

There is real power in a manifesto. What you say to yourself and to others has an impact on the world. You can harness that power and turn it inward to influence and recruit your best self. To keep yourself both motivated and mindful throughout this work, you'll want to cultivate two important mindsets that help form the boundaries of this work: agency and humility.

Step in with Grace

Agency is the power to effect change, make decisions, implement ideas, and achieve goals. It is the ability to act, unhindered by physical or structural blocks. Agency is also the *feeling* of the ability to act, that internal permission to pursue and achieve. It carries the meaning of both "can" and "may." You need agency—both the feeling of it in order to act and the fact of it in order to make change.

Right now, agency is unevenly distributed—some people have much more access to power than others. But in some important ways, it is more available than ever. Even if you don't think of yourself as a designer, we are all punching above our weight as creators with just the smartphones in our pockets. While there are significant structural blocks to power for many people that prevent them from exercising their intentions directly, we also have more capacity and access than ever to lift each other up and give each other permission to act and make the change we need.

We all need to feel the power and joy of acting in the face of challenge and opportunity. But we also need humility and restraint to ensure that we guard against hubris and harm. Many of the creative tools that we use now are technologies based on sophisticated research, new manipulations of human behavior that allow unproven ideas to be scaled so fast and far that they affect hundreds of millions of people in real ways before we even know what they are (prechecked boxes for monthly donations on one-time digital forms, anyone?). Creative work is more viral than ever—and that capacity is amoral. It can work for good. But you, as an individual, have to be the one to bring the sense of moral judgment to bear. This requires humility.

Humility feeds awareness and leads to a posture of learning, seeking to grow in skill and do better in the future by understanding and reflecting on past and present work. You can't ask for more than that. Humility acknowledges that we don't know everything about what we have invented and that intentions are not the same as outcomes.

Humility does not mean inaction. We can and should be working on even the most difficult problems and sensitive topics, and a strong set of ethics and values can help guide you in those endeavors, as well as in situations that are less risky and delicate. By spending time to understand your motivations, biases, and reservations, you will be better equipped to make the best decisions you can at any given moment; to get in there and get to work with gusto—and a manifesto.

Craft Your Way to a Manifesto

You don't have to become a radical philosopher or avant-garde artist to produce a great manifesto. You can make a manifesto that works for you and helps you make solid choices when it counts, using just a few simple tools and processes.

The hands-on, design-based exercises in this book will guide you to make your first manifesto by borrowing the wisdom of others. All you need to do is open your eyes and ears and gather some simple office supplies—yes, you read that right: you'll be using paper, scissors, and glue—and tuning in to your very fine sense of independent judgment. Lean into your intuition. Play, practice, and prototype your way to clarity and conviction.

To build your manifesto, you will begin with a deliberate process of actively examining your values and beliefs. Once you've done this inner work you will move outward, mindfully collecting the raw material for your manifesto in the inspiring words of others. There are countless pieces of wisdom, statements of purpose, manifestos, mantras, and memes available to you from designers, artists, writers, scientists, philosophers, religious leaders, social activists, and more.

Next, you'll synthesize and filter this material through your own experience and for your own understanding to make it true for you. And finally, you will curate this collected wisdom into an expression of your own, a living document that you can trust and test and change. Over time, this work will teach you how to identify and merge your knowledge, feelings, and beliefs into an assured sense of self-awareness. Defining your manifesto will give you a clear understanding and crisp articulation of the goals you're moving toward, the values that drive you, and the ethics that govern the boundaries of your work.

Crafting a manifesto is a simple exercise, and it works. There's no single perfect way to do it. Instead, there are many. Your manifesto can be about your aspirations and intentions; it can be about your convictions and your goals; it can be about your behaviors, your identity, or your impact in the world. It is a practice of self-awareness—part of a set of key skills that everyone can benefit from, whether you call yourself a designer or not.

THE ACT OF CAPTURING IS CAPTURING TO ACT.

A MANIFESTO IS A STATEMENT OF

CONSIDER
YOUR
POSITION

(UN)PACK
YOUR BAG

GOALS VALUES ETHICS BIAS

COLLECT

WISDOM
FROM ANYWHERE

AND **INSPIRATION** FROM EVERYWHERE

honor
your
sources

inform
your
intuition

let it steep

KEEP YOUR EYES & EARS OPEN

PURPOSE & A SCRIPT FOR ACTION

form and
style matter.

work your framework

SAY IT LIKE
YOU MEAN IT.

&

CURATE

IT'S YOUR
MANIFESTO.

TRUST IT
& TEST IT

REFLECT &
RENEW IT.

REFLECT &
RENEW IT

CULTIVATE IT
WITH OTHERS

KEEP YOUR SELF & SOUL OPEN

2.2) ☐ Lists for others are easy; sequencing is difficult.

3.2) ☐ 100% of this is planning; the rest is doing.

4.2) ☐ Conscript the most capable into your army; challenge them and reward them, and challenge them again.

5.2) ☐ Have boundaries. Know them. Share them often.

6.2) ☐ Harm no one. Humanize your opposition.

* Completion of this form is compulsory and
performing of each function is a necessary
step toward your own liberation from what
ails you, holds you back, or cramps your
style. Best results when performed in numer-
ical progression.

Signed: _____

Witnessed: _____

CONSIDER

*

›So, you are ready to
make a revolution?‹

1.2) ☐   If any more than two people need
to have fun there must be a plan.

Take an Inner Road Trip

To recruit yourself, you need to know yourself. A practice of self-awareness equips every maker, creator, or problem solver with an essential understanding of their own relationship to the process of getting work done. Know yourself, and everything will work better.

So, before you seek inspiration for your manifesto from other people, let's do some internal warmups to become familiar with a few key parts of your system of moral navigation: your goals, values, ethics, and biases. I've already compared your manifesto to a compass; in this landscape, you might think of goals as your destinations, values as the gas you need to get there, ethics as your steering wheel, and biases as well-worn paths and ruts in the roads. The exercises in this chapter will help you find and express all four of these components.

Get to Know Your Destinations

Goals are destinations. The journey to them can be more short-term, like "write this book," or more long-term, like "bring up my kids to become healthy, thoughtful, productive adults." They are a conceptualization of a place, a moment, or a state of being where you want to arrive. In our daily grind, it's not always easy to see what goals we are actively pursuing. You've got to stop the hustle for a minute to get a look at the goals worth reaching.

Arriving at a goal often brings a sense of achievement, closure, and satisfaction, whereas missing the mark can feel like failure, frustration, and loss. Equally, although navigating without a destination can feel freeing in the short term, in the long term a lack of purpose can produce feelings of aimlessness and defeat. Goals are a great way to plot a deliberate course through your life and work. However, as with all things set in the future, we need to regularly reexamine that course in relation to the present.

As my colleagues Andrea Small and Kelly Schmutte have said in their book, *Navigating Ambiguity,* wayfinding is a matter of paying attention—cultivating awareness of where you are and what is happening. You may have a destination in mind, but there are many ways to get to that destination. And as you are finding your way there, new destinations may beckon more strongly. So though a goal gives you direction and structure for your journey, it's not always where you end up.

Taking time to consider your goals—the ones you'd like to have as well as the ones that you're actively pursuing— can help orient you toward work that is meaningful to you and that you want to do well. The only way to truly know your goals is to look inward. Get to know yourself. Dig around to see what goals you might already have in your backpack.

Ask Why

One way to begin to craft a worthy goal is to look at the things you are already doing today and see what those actions can tell you about the goals you are already pursuing and the ones you are not. Start by making some lists to answer these questions. They may seem simple, but you'll be surprised by where they will lead you.

> **What did you do yesterday, and what are you planning to do today?**

> **What did you do last weekend, and what are you planning to do this weekend?**

> **What are some things you're looking forward to or hoping for?**

Now, look at each of your answers and ask *why?* Why did you do those things? Why are you planning to do that? Why are you looking forward to it? The answer to each new question should start with the phrase "Because I . . ." (It's important that the "I" is in there.)

Once you've written down all of your "Because I" answers, you can start looking for the kernels of your current goals in these statements that start after the word "because." First, you'll find phrases like "I want," "I need," "I care about," "I'm worried that," "I'm excited about." And right after that, you'll likely find an interesting phrase that points to something you hope to achieve. This is the kernel of an existing goal or value. Take a look at it and see if you can articulate it. If it's not quite there, you might need to ask *why* again, and answer "Because I . . ." Eventually, you'll get to something that speaks to your deeper desires and motivations.

Yesterday I . . .

> **Wrote part of my book—because I want to deliver it on time. (I want to deliver it on time because even though I fail at this all the time, I still want to be the kind of person you can count on.)**

Today I . . .

Last weekend I . . .

This weekend I . . .

I'm looking forward to, I'm hoping for . . .

Some of the goals you are actively pursuing, especially today and tomorrow, will feel a bit mundane. That's good; we all have to put food on the table. But there is deeper meaning behind those things you do. Also, you might just as easily find that what you do and why you do it are two different things. That's also where you want to go. For instance, if you look at the example response I gave here, there is a contradiction in my answer. Contradictions equal aspirations. Aspiration is the gap between what you do and what you want to do. Thinking about what you want to be known for (but aren't yet known for) is a landmark for a goal. It's a lighthouse lighting the way around the rocky shores of your bad habits.

Are there things you're looking forward to or hoping for that feel more inspiring? Take a look at your list of proto-goals and ask yourself:

> **What's missing from this list that I know I care about?**
>
> **What do I secretly wish I was doing instead?**
>
> **What have I always wanted to do that's not on this list?**

This exercise—and the others in this book—is about getting started. This list of proto-goals is not an endpoint; it's a way to wake up your system and get interested in examining what you care about and what you want. You've got to step out of your grind to examine why you do the things you do. If you ask *why?* enough times, you'll get to your true goals and what you truly value.

Put Gas in the Tank

Values are simply what you value in your life. They help
you determine what is important to you in both the long
term and the short. These underlying beliefs influence your
behavior and motivate your actions—the ones you take
and the ones you don't take. Some are derived from your
personal experiences, some you inherit from your family
or your culture, and others you adopt as a part of your
learning. Your values are changeable. What is of value to
you today may not be in ten years. (In fact, let's hope not.)
Your values are also personal. I can't tell you what values to
have—they are yours, not mine. What I can tell you is that
you need them. Why? It's gas in the tank. **Values motivate
you.** They push you. Let them. Get good at letting them push
you.

Values matter because they are present in everything we
do, but they also hide in our actions—they are not always
self-evident and not often self-examined. By airing your
values as part of the work of creating your manifesto, you
have the opportunity to examine and evolve your sense of
purpose as you gain experience and wisdom.

A swift search for "personal values" on the internet will
get you a huge number of lists of "values to live by." In any
of these lists, you'll probably recognize and resonate with
some of the values listed, while some may feel like they
don't fit with your outlook or your work. Some may feel
more aspirational than actual, and some might actually

be hard to differentiate from one another. For me, the problem is that they have no reference to anything real in my life. They're ideas up in the air, shifting and moving around like clouds—not practical, not grounded in reality, action, and behavior.

One way to bring these airy concepts down to earth is to sneak up on them by examining your daily pursuits as a way to discover what you value beyond the obvious. Start with the behaviors, actions, and objects that are important to you and extract your values from them. In the previous exercise, you may have discovered some of your values just by asking *why* a few times. This particular exercise will ask you to look for them by telling stories and using metaphors.

Your Love Is Like a Red Red Rose*

Even though I hate the feeling of dirt under my fingernails, plants are a puzzle that I just love to try and solve. I love to see the way plants grow—it is actual magic unfolding in front of me.

I also love to make things; from sewing, knitting, and leatherworking to glassblowing, metalsmithing, and pottery. I love to understand how processes work. I love the feeling of making something truly beautiful and practical. I love the craft of it all.

I can see that I enjoy and thrive in the act of gardening and making. I know that I value them, but without further investigation, that's where it might end. But these loved activities are the key to uncovering my values.

Consider what you love to do. To pull some deeper meaning out of your treasured pursuits, chronicle what you care about by using some strategic metaphors or similes. This is a technique designers use all the time. By testing comparisons and associations between two concepts, you can create a new understanding of your pursuits and goals and why they are important to you. Metaphors and similes highlight particular (and sometimes peculiar) meanings through comparison. Sometimes they click, other times they don't. But when one clicks, it lets you see something that you think of as normal in a totally new way, and that can help you change course.

*with gratitude to the poet Robert Burns

First, write down a very short description of something you do that you truly love, as I just did with gardening. You can get a little flowery about it (see what I did there?), explaining all the little reasons why you love it, all the moments that you savor, the triumphs and the tribulations.

Next, look at the following list and begin associating your loved activity, one by one.

   **My loved activity**   is like   _**a metaphor**_   because
    **a reason** .

Search your mind to find an association between the two ideas. Try hard! But if you can't find anything, move on to the next one. Some similes will be really fruitful, some less so. Keep going until you get to the end of the list.

   Gardening is like a giraffe . . . **Hmm, nothing comes to mind here . . .**

   Gardening is like a river **because I can float in it peacefully.**

   Gardening is like a clock **because it reminds me of the cyclical and the eternal.**

   Gardening is like a peppermint **because it wakes me up, makes me feel fresh and well.**

Take a look at what you've written. Can you pick out some specific words that give you a clue to what you might value about the concept you've described? Highlight them.

Look at all your highlighted words and try them on for size. Interrogate them. Which ones do you care about the most? Why? Write a bit about each one to see if it leads you to another.

Finally, compare the words you've highlighted to the list of common core values below and pick out the ones that correspond. What stands out? What is a surprise to you? What feels like it is missing?

This exercise is a way to spark awareness about the things that you care about. The truth is, if you are not following a course prescribed by your own values, you are likely subscribing to someone else's, and that can quickly lead to both a sense of purposelessness and weak or nonexistent ethics. Don't get hijacked by corporate pirates; sail an algorithm of your own instead.

An Extremely Short List of Core Values

Authenticity	Curiosity	Love
Achievement	Determination	Loyalty
Adventure	Faith	Optimism
Autonomy	Friendships	Recognition
Balance	Fun	Respect
Beauty	Growth	Responsibility
Boldness	Honesty	Security
Compassion	Influence	Service
Citizenship	Justice	Status
Competency	Kindness	Wisdom

Where's the Steering Wheel on This Thing?

I love ethics. Especially when it comes to creative work. Especially when that creative work comes with the powder-keg combination of endless human imagination, the tools of design, and the unfathomable scope of emerging technologies. Right now, formal training in any one of these fields does not involve much in the way of restraint and guidance. We need to change that.

If values are the accelerator for driving toward your goals, then ethics are more like the brakes, the steering, or the lines on the road. Ethics are the rules and restraints we establish for ourselves to keep from running all over the place, squashing everything that's in our path. Without an accepted set of rules of the road, you can struggle to know how and where to stop, especially when your vehicle can take you far beyond where it's safe to go.

It is a bit weird to say "I love ethics." It's like saying "I love brakes." But they are useful when you need them, and worthy of your affection. If we spent more time loving the things that protect us, we would spend less time hurting ourselves.

Ethics are your rules, whether they are personal guides to your own behavior or a collective set of laws that keep all of us on paths safely. Built in line with your values and responsive to your experiences, they indicate your boundaries and the ways you get to your destination.

They govern the behavior you've decided is okay and the types of actions that you want to avoid. Ethics prevent us from doing and saying things that are contrary to our values, that we know we will regret.

In the past few years, a variety of people have worked to develop and distribute a more robust set of ethics for the fields of design, technology, and creative work overall. While you may not think of yourself as a designer, your work is most definitely adding to the world. In that respect, we are all designers, and every one of us needs a steering wheel and decent brakes.

These are excellent resources to help you begin to determine the ethics that should make it into your personal manifesto, but there's still plenty of room for your contribution. As you are creating your manifesto, use the opportunity to ask yourself if there are any guardrails in there, any brakes, any limits. If you've got your personal ethics in place, you'll be better able to tell when you, your organization, or your field is heading in the wrong direction.

The Ruts in the Road

Biases are the predetermined preferences that we hold; they can be favored routes to travel—or ruts in the road. So often we make choices based on instinct, but it is important to understand and examine the ways in which your preferences have developed. Great goals are rarely achieved by following a predetermined course. Understanding your preferences can help you see where you need to push through unnecessary or unjust boundaries imposed by convention, negative influences, and systemic or structural prejudice.

Biases are tendencies to favor or disfavor anything based on your previous experiences or cultural norms. **Everyone has biases—they are a product of a learning brain.** They form because the brain categorizes new experiences based on prior knowledge. Our brain connects new ideas, new people, and new things to categories we've formed from all of our earlier experiences and then responds to them the same way it does to other things in that category. This means that we have all had personal experiences and been exposed to cultural norms that are influencing our decisions and actions based on bias.

While some of these biases are very useful (to keep us from walking into oncoming traffic) and some are harmless (like "sour cream and onion chips are just better than barbecue"), some are incredibly harmful both to others and to ourselves. Stereotypes passed to us from our families, the cultures we grew up in or are living in, and

DESIGN ETHICS
A 21ST CENTURY PRIMER

A Designer's Code of Ethics
Mike Monteiro, Mule Design

An Introductory Ethic for Designers
Rick Griffith, Matter

A Designer's Critical Alphabet
**Lesley-Ann Noel,
Pluriversal Design Lab**

The Ethical Operating System
Institute for the Future

Inclusive Design Methodology
Microsoft

The Tarot Cards of Tech
and *Humanity-Centered Design*
Artefact Group

Liberatory Design Methods
**Tania Anaissie,
Victor Cary, David Clifford,
Tom Malarky, Susie Wise**

the media and information we consume can predetermine our ideas about ourselves and other people based on race, cultural background, religion, gender, sexual orientation, and so much more. They can make us jump to conclusions about other people's values, beliefs, ethics, and goals.

Prior experiences or teachings from people we respect can form locked attitudes toward new experiences and new people that predispose us to judge them based on only this earlier knowledge. While it's not possible to live a life with no biases at all, it is critical to know that they exist, to become aware of what yours are, and to bring them into the light so you can spend time and effort to change when you need to. By exposing your implicit biases, you can make more deliberate choices.

Louie Montoya, design lead for the K12 Lab at the d.school, maintains that examining bias is mostly about asking simple questions about where your ideas come from. By realizing that they are intertwined with your own personal beliefs, experiences, and trauma, you can make a difference in the way you think. If you dig into some of the things that you do every day and understand where those behaviors come from, it's easier to ask *What other bigger beliefs do I have? How does that influence me and the power I have in the world?* As Louie shared with me:

Ask yourself, *Who am I? If I'm operating from this position, can I just make that position more visible for myself?* Ask yourself, *What kinds of unrealized mechanisms are operating in me that make something feel good or feel scary, or make me feel certain ways? Where did they come from, and what does that mean?*

Seven Lenses

Here is an activity adapted from the Design for Worldview workshop created by Emi Kolawole and Amy Lazarus in 2016 at the d.school. It's a lovely introspective way to explore the gaps between the stories that you tell yourself about your life. Get yourself a pencil and some paper, and get ready to tell a story.

First, describe seven lenses through which you see the world. A lens is an attribute you have that is part of the way you define yourself or your identity. It may be your gender, religion, geographic origin, family role, career, and more. For each one, describe how and when you became aware of this lens in your life.

Now think about an encounter you had with someone in your life that was uncomfortable. Choose a moment that was an interaction: someone else besides you must have been involved in the moment. Write a short account of this interaction, what was said or done, and how you felt about it.

Next, choose one lens from your seven lenses and share more details about this experience through the lens you chose. For example . . .

> **As a mother I felt protective when I was in the presence of a stranger with my children, but I also wanted to be a good role model for them, to not avoid a difficult situation that might require a compassionate approach.**

Choose another lens and write your impressions about the encounter from that perspective. Keep going until you are out of lenses or out of time.

Finally, use a noun to fill in this phrase:

If I looked at this experience from the perspective of _____, I might learn something new.

And then use a verb to fill in this phrase:

I could _____ to learn more about this new perspective.

Telling the story from each additional perspective reveals a slightly different set of assumptions about the way in which you approach the world. It's not hard to extrapolate how varied the experience would look from a whole other set of eyes or circumstances. This is the kind of practice that expands your awareness of your bias. In developing your manifesto, you will benefit from this kind of alternate perspective-taking as a careful balance to your instinctive choices.

Get on with It

All this talk of values and ethics and goals can make this project seem like the stakes are too high. You might be worrying, *What if I can't identify my values? What if I don't have the "right" goals?* If you are worrying, it's okay. The beauty of the approach you are about to take is in its flexibility. You're not setting anything in stone. Your first manifesto is going to be a prototype, and so is your second and your third. Free yourself from any sense of obligation— you don't owe anyone anything. Trust your intuition. There's only one person your manifesto can and needs to be totally true for, and that is you, right now. In the next chapter, you will get to spend some time looking outside of yourself for inspiration. Learning from others is one of the key skills that designers cultivate, and this moment is no exception.

DETERMINED COMPASSIONATE
BEINGS—WHO LOVE
AND LEARN AND LISTEN FOR
OPPORTUNITIES T BEAT BACK INDIFFERENCE
AND PREJUDICE.
TRY NOT TO DISAPPOINT
WITH HALF MEASURES AND

STUDENT NONVIOLENT
COORDINATING COMMITTEE
WE SHALL OVERCOME

LACKLUSTER LEANINGS.

HERE,
WE ARE ALL THE
WAY IN - ALL THE
WAY ALIVE.

Rick Griffith

COLLECT

WELCOME TO THIS STRUGGLE. THE FIGHT ISN'T NEW – THE FIGHTERS ARE. HERE WE GET TO LINK ARMS WITH SOME OF THE MOST NOBLE AND IMPECCABLE HUMANS IN OUR HISTORY. HERE WE ARE RESILIENT

Inspiration Comes from the Outside

You are going to begin creating a manifesto of your own by borrowing wisdom—deliberately looking for manifestos, guidance, prescriptions, and other texts written by people who have gone through their own process to distill wisdom out of their experiences. You will use these sources as the base material for creating an understanding of your own attitudes.

The roots of the word *inspiration* mean to "breathe in" or "to be breathed into." I take that as a directive. When I'm most frustrated and stuck and stymied, I have to step back and take a deep breath, inhaling new information— mental oxygen—to change my perspective. Inspiration is often parodied as a eureka moment that arrives out of nowhere, without warning or preparation, to people who are somehow endowed with extra talent, gifts, or luck that you don't have. But there is another type of inspiration that everyone has experience with, one that doesn't require any special talent or magic moment: learning from others. You need oxygen to breathe and oxygen to light a fire. The inspiration you glean from others is your oxygen for this project, and the fuel you will use to get rolling is other people's experience and wisdom. What a relief to know that inspiration is in the air all around us.

Many wise and wonderful people have found for themselves the same kind of guidance that you are looking for. You have access to vast sources of inspiration. People who have worked and experienced and synthesized and imagined and written down words to help you to understand something they themselves had come to know. These people have taken the time and effort to collect their work and write it down so that you could benefit from it. They published these works to get them out in the world, to teach and influence others. It is your job to find them, to process them, to learn from the works, and transform them for yourself. You are going to **take these gifts with gratitude** and use their manifestos, statements of purpose, lyrics, essays, and more as a starting place for your own manifesto.

Honor Your Sources

Where will you find all this amazing inspiration? Keep your ears and eyes open. Keep your self and soul open. You can collect wisdom from anywhere and inspiration from everywhere. How will you know it's the right stuff? It's what feels right to you, right now. Dig into manifestos from design, philosophy, social justice, biology, environmental science, business, law, art, medicine, fiction, food, religion, lyrics, poetry, lyric poetry, whatever floats your boat. You might be attracted to the person who made the piece because of what you know of their life or their work, or it might be the work itself that speaks to you. It could even be a situation that you want to capture. Maybe the text doesn't mean as much to you as the memory of the moment when you encountered it, when it helped you crystallize a particular thought or idea or memorialize a moment of learning or of deep value to you.

When you learn from others, you take in the words, ideas, and examples they have offered, process them through your own experience, and create a new understanding for yourself. To make your manifesto, you're going to externalize that process, to make it happen on the outside of your head—so you can see it as it takes shape in front of you—and to make it easy to work with. And while you are free to find and learn from and use the work of others to create your own understanding, you have a responsibility to your sources.

Behind every source of inspiration that you find is an actual person:
A real human who did the work to understand their world and save wisdom for themself and others. That is hard work. Acknowledge it. Seek your sources; find out who they are or were. Explore their work and understand more about them. Reading is learning from teachers who are always there for you. Express your gratitude to them. Be authentic. Steal like an artist. Acknowledge and refer, appreciate and learn. Borrow from your sources with grace and reverence. Give credit where credit is due, and make it your own truth.

BE A WIDE FUNNEL WITH A SMALL HOLE. BE CHOOSY.

Gather It In

Although in theory you can find the raw material for your manifesto anywhere and everywhere, in practice it can be overwhelming and ineffective. Let's narrow the field. You're going to start with some concise statements, not too many of them, all of them written by other people.

Your task is to find ten inspiring sources of wisdom, guidance, and advice that appeal to you and apply to the work you do. Each one stands as an example of the collected wisdom of its writer or writers. These can be pointedly prescriptive and historical, like manifestos, pieces of professional guidance, statements of purpose, or open letters and essays. Or they can be more oblique and artful, like poems, lyrics, narrative fiction, or drama. This is *your* search, of course, so you should follow your own curiosity, but I'm not going to leave you without a few places to start. In addition to my own ten sources, here are a few things to consider as you begin your search.

Harvest your field

First, look for work by people in your field that you admire. What are you passionate about? What are you studying? The list I use comes mostly from the field of design and art because those are fields I spend most of my time engaging in. But you should bring in the writers, leaders, researchers, artists, or whoever else is important to you.

Get outside your bubble

Second, do the opposite. Try to go outside the bubbles
of your field, your institutions, and your cultures and
look around. Be interdisciplinary and expansive. Include
material that is about life, fun, and play in addition to
work, ethics, and commitments.

What are you learning?

Many of the d.school's teaching teams who run the
manifesto project—yes, it's a class!—hand out a page
of all the most recently taught concepts or takeaways
for their students to incorporate into their manifesto,
cementing their learning into a guide for new behaviors
or mindsets. What is something you have been studying
lately? Be it cooking or rock climbing, philosophy or
statistics, pull in some of your most recently acquired
ideas, skills, and advice.

Finally, be choosy. You'll cast your net wide to begin with.
But in the end, you need to settle on the few pieces that
you want to use, more than five but fewer than ten. Save
the rest of them for a second, third, or fourth round. Your
pile of primary sources should be compact enough to read
through comfortably in less than an hour.

Make your sources physical

Many of your sources will be found as digital images or texts on the internet. Some may be from books or other types of media or material. To accomplish the next step, you need to get all of them onto pieces of paper so that you can harvest from them easily with a pair of scissors. Printing them out or copying them on a copy machine works best, but if you don't have access to a printer you can capture what you need by hand-copying, writing, or drawing. When it comes to curating your work later, you might choose to use a digital medium to present it—cutting and pasting digitally can work if you are really familiar with those kinds of tools—but for most people, the more physical you can make it, the better it will feel.

If you need a kick-start, here's a list of sources that I have used for the manifesto project at the d.school. You can use these to begin your search for the raw material for your manifesto. My sources lean heavy into art and design, because that's what I'm most excited by. These are by no means the only sources of inspiration you should use to determine what you believe, but they are a place to start if you need one.

SOURCES I USE

Immaculate Heart College
Art Department Rules
by Corita Kent

An Incomplete Manifesto for Growth
by Bruce Mau

Ten Principles for Good Design
by Deiter Rams

Steal Like an Artist
by Austin Kleon

Some Things I've Learned
in My Life So Far
by Stefan Sagmeister

The BlackSpace Manifesto
by BlackSpace Urbanist Collective

The Design Abilities
by Carissa Carter

An Introductory Ethic for Designers
by Rick Griffith

Last Lemon Manifesto
by Lisa Swerling
and Ralph Lazar

100 Quotes by Charles Eames
Edited by Carla Hatman
and Eames Demetrios

SOURCES OF SOURCES

100+ Years of Design Manifestos, backspace.com, John Emerson

The Marginalian, themarginalian.org, Maria Popova

NITCH, nitch.com, Anonymous

Inform Your Intuition

Now that you have your sources of inspiration in front of you, the next step is to look inside these texts for the good stuff to harvest for your manifesto. How will you decide what to take from the material you have? You're going to see what resonates and not think too much about it.

We're all equipped with two very robust systems for determining what it is that we believe. The first and most powerful is an involuntary, instinctive, intuitive, emotional system. We all know the idea that you can make a "gut" decision, but recent research has begun to help us understand just how powerfully emotional all decision making and belief creation is. You'll use that tendency to your advantage when collecting selections for your manifesto from the raw material you've assembled. Afterward, when curating, you'll bring the second system— the conscious, rational, frontal lobe type thinking—back into the picture to discern and critique, prioritize, and coordinate.

In his book *Thinking, Fast and Slow,* Daniel Kahneman beautifully describes the way these two systems interact:

> **System 1 operates automatically and quickly, with little or no effort and no sense of voluntary control. System 2 allocates attention to the effortful mental activities that demand it, including complex computations. The operations of System 2 are often**

associated with the subjective experience of agency, choice, and concentration.

Systems 1 and 2 are both active whenever we are awake. System 1 continuously generates suggestions for System 2: impressions, intuitions, intentions, and feelings. If endorsed by System 2, impressions and intuitions turn into beliefs, and impulses turn into voluntary actions.

When we think of ourselves, we identify with System 2, the conscious, reasoning self that has beliefs, makes choices, and decides what to think about and what to do. Although System 2 believes itself to be where the action is, the automatic System 1 is the hero . . . effortlessly originating impressions and feelings that are the main sources of the explicit beliefs and deliberate choices of System 2.

System 1 is, to some extent, trained to react by our biology, but also by practice, association, and experience. We can take the results of our more deliberate System 2 thoughts and internalize them, encoding them to become a System 1 reaction with practice or repetition over time. This is how we inform our intuition and build the leanings and preferences that we often call instinct. It's also how we form our biases. What's great about this is that the fact that we've acquired many of our instinctive reactions through training means we can retrain them too.

This is why it's so important to get your manifesto out of your head and out in front of you. Making the process deliberate allows you to actively engage both of these systems. Collecting inspiration and material using System 1 shows you what you already believe, and questioning it with System 2 lets you build new beliefs, add new information to the mix, and reprogram System 1.

To make decisions about what to take from your collected raw material, you are going to lean on System 1 thinking. You'll be looking for a reaction that is more emotional than rational. It is often described as resonance, a sense of affinity, or recognition that you have when you encounter something that aligns with your values and beliefs.

COLLECT TO ASPIRE.
WE SHOULD ALL GET BETTER.
COLLECT TO ENCOURAGE.
WE ALL NEED IT.
COLLECT TO REMEMBER.
THERE ARE SOME THINGS
WE SHOULD NOT
FORGET.

Sound It Out

Put your packet of printed materials in front of you. With your scissors at the ready, begin to read. As you read through your collected manifestos, missives, and mantras, notice the statements that you are attracted to. When you read something that you feel is true for you, collect it by cutting it out with your scissors. Put some time into this, but don't overthink it. It should take less than an hour for you to look through your sources and collect a pile of statements that resonates with you.

Ring your bell

Think of your goals, values, and ethics as your bell. Use your System 1 thinking and pay attention to how you feel as you explore the works you've chosen. What rings true to you? When you find something on your frequency, capture it, copy it, cut it out, and put it into the collection pile.

You are looking for statements to which you have an emotional reaction. It could be positive (resonance) or negative (dissonance), but it should have some amplitude. No "meh" statements. Most of the statements you collect will have a positive resonance, which might feel like an affinity, a sense of rightness or truth, or an urge to remember or hold onto a statement or an idea. When it's negative, it could feel like a provocation, an itch, anger, or an urge to amend, tweak, reframe, or change. Does it ring a sour note? Grapple with it, and see if you might want to counter it with a reaction of your own. If it engages you, capture it and keep it in your pile to work with later.

The act of collecting might be an affirmation of your experience, an aspiration to new behaviors, or a need to challenge accepted wisdom. The statements you harvest could be about process, actions, and behaviors or about mindsets, beliefs, and values. In fact, it's great to capture a wide variety of types of statements. If you've got wisdom of your own, from a notebook or in your head, write it out on an empty patch of paper and cut it out.

Get messy and have fun

Give yourself some space. Sit on the floor or at a big table that's not too formal or precious. (It's hard to be too serious about what you're working on when you're sitting on the floor, and you'll need a playful attitude.) Spread your material out in front of you to work with. These sources are the basis of your work, but right now they are not precious. To get what you need from them, you really have to treat them as raw material, ready to be shredded and reconstituted by you.

If you do work on a small desk or table, pile the bits you collect in front of you and let all the rest fall to the floor. However you go about it, it's essential to approach it with a spirit of play. Getting too serious about it all will engage your System 2 thinking too soon. If you overthink your choices in the beginning, your instincts won't have a chance to tell you anything, and you'll get stuck in deliberation. Curating is your next step; trust that you'll be able to make another decision about it then.

At the end of thirty or forty minutes, you should have a pile of precious cut paper in front of you and another pile of stuff on the floor all around you, ready to be recycled.

Move from Instinct to Insight

Now is the time to move from thinking fast to thinking slow—to make some connections and build some hunches about the meaning of your instinctive choices. The d.school's director of teaching and learning, Carissa Carter, often describes this activity as *stewing*—that period when all the main ingredients are present, but the flavor of the final dish hasn't yet developed. It takes both time and energy to simmer the stew into deliciousness. I'm a lover of herbal teas, so I call it *steeping*, but it's a similar idea. Tea requires a medium—water—to hydrate all the raw ingredients, the energy of heat to extract and develop their fragrance and flavor, and time to mix them all together and let them gain strength.

In this next step, you'll be processing all the information you have collected and putting it together with your lived experience and understanding. Smushing things together like this will create new associations and lead to new insights about what you value and believe. These insights are key for creating a manifesto that is tailored to you—to your experience, your talents, your aspirations, your hopes and dreams, and your goals and worries. During this step, things should feel like they are coming together. Still, leave plenty of room for discovery, as messing about with meaning always creates new opportunities.

You might be tempted to randomly attach your collection of clippings to a page without due consideration. But don't skip the steeping step. You'll just end up with weak tea.

Steep

Look over the pile of statements you have collected. Spread it out so you can get a good overview of what you have and still be able to move the statements around.

Start to look for commonalities. Group together statements that seem to have a connection to one another. See if you can come up with a headline or label for each group, and write each down on a scrap of paper. Break up the groups and do another round, again looking for different common themes. Try again, this time looking for contrasts or contradictions, and label these as well. Save all the labels, adding them to your collection of statements.

As you arrange and rearrange your collection, think about the statements in relation to the goals and values that you have already brought to light. Ask yourself a few questions and capture your answers as well.

What kinds of actions, attitudes, and behaviors do the statements that you captured suggest? List them.

Do the statements you've collected support the values and goals you found earlier? Do they venture into totally new territory? Do they contradict those earlier findings? What does that say about your current relationship with your values and goals?

How do the statements relate to one another? Are there patterns emerging? What kinds of insights about your goals and values can you draw from any patterns?

Does part of your collection provoke dissonance or disagreement? Do you want to redirect or restate something in another way? Amend any statements to reflect what you believe.

The good news is you can take some time to do this part. And whatever time you can spare will be worthwhile. You can start this work, putting a bit of energy into arranging and rearranging, and then, if you like, let it sit for a while before coming back to it. Some of the best steeping happens in your subconscious, while you are sleeping or in the shower or making dinner or tying your shoes. Or you can power through it, think a lot, answer a lot of questions, and move on to the next step. The steeping will still be happening—in fact, it will accelerate—as you begin to curate your manifesto.

FOR THE BRAVE LIBRARIAN, EACH ACT OPENS AN INTERDIMENSIONAL...

EACH ACT... EACH OTHER... BACKWATERD PERSO... A FORGED...

OPENING PORTALS IS A [P]... REVOLUTIONARY ACTS. E... BEHIND YOU. PULL... BE... TO SHARE. ALWAYS IN LOVE AN... STUDENT. THERE HAS ALWAYS... IN LOVE... CRAFTED... THEY ARE IN... ALWAYS... ARE NEVE... ME. ... NOW TIME... OTHERS... IN STRUGGL... FORWARD. DEFINING TIME. OF YOU AND... A PERSON AND A... ACHANCE AND A... ...SIONAL PORTAL. ...ST SCHOLAR. THE VORACIOUS

Rick Griffith

4

CURATE

Say It Like You Mean It

You should now have a bountiful pile of stuff to work with that you have collected, considered, steeped in, and added to. With your pile, you have some insights and hunches or questions about the patterns of your choices and how they relate to some of your motivations and goals. How can you answer those questions and explore those hunches, while at the same time creating something you can show to other people? It's time to curate.

Curating is the intentional selection, organization, and presentation of objects in a collection. On the surface, curating is about organizing ideas and objects into a visual presentation that communicates meaning to others. And a good presentation is often the result of a successful curation process. But in this situation, curating is first and foremost about having an open conversation with yourself, full of both curiosity and introspection.

The root of the word *curation* is *curare,* meaning "to take care of." As part of this process, you'll explore different frameworks and formats to organize and transform your pile of collected statements into your manifesto. What form speaks to you and speaks for you to others? This will be the framework for your manifesto, and it will provide a model for the further selection and organization of your material. I'll be giving you one quick and easy first method for presenting your manifesto, but you'll also play with alternative ways of presenting your work, to see how it changes the meaning of your words.

The goal of this is to work your work—to actively process your thoughts, ideas, feelings, questions, and convictions in full view, creating a personal feedback loop that helps you to develop an authentic personal point of view. By investigating the relationships among the items you have chosen, pushing your thinking outside of yourself, you will create test narratives: potential affinities, contrasts, and other associations to put through your feedback loop, building an organizing structure of your very own. You'll continue your hands-on work to find the right time, place, and medium to present your manifesto, and you'll learn how to maintain it as a living document of your learning and growth.

Work Your Framework

You have already begun using frameworks to create meaning for yourself. The brief grouping and pattern-finding you did to hunt for insights and questions is an example of a loose framework. Frameworks are really just methods of organizing. Like scaffolding, they allow you to support the thing you are building while it is still in progress. For a manifesto, a framework can influence how you say what you want to say—both the tone and the organizing principle. Do you want the Ten Commandments or a top ten list? An essay or an epigram? A mantra or a metaphor? Serious, irreverent, poetic, prosaic?

Examples of frameworks to help you organize your manifesto are available in the manifestos you've been using as your raw material. You'll see everything from letters and lists to diagrams and infographic maps. You can look beyond those examples too for other frameworks that might interest you. Some are highly structured, with hierarchies and orders; others are much looser, flatter, and more casual. Think about what kind of framework might suit you, your work, or your context best.

For some people, a starter structure is a really useful tool. If you're the kind of person who likes to have a worksheet to fill in or a recipe to follow, try choosing a structure that appeals to you and see if your collection can fit in it well. But if you're less sure about what kind of framework could

A FRAMEWORK SPECTRUM

MORE

Top five/ten/etc. lists

Principles or rules

Platforms
(political or otherwise)

Metaphors
(a solar system, a baseball
game, a landscape, an organism)

Maps

FAQs

Poetry or lyric structures

Letter (to your future self or to the editor)

Advice or opinion column

Epigrams or slogans

Word clouds

LESS

work for you, especially for your first prototype, you might want to allow yourself to remain on the looser side of this spectrum, constructing the content of your manifesto without too much concern for how it will be organized or connected. As you work your work, you'll find that over time it adopts the structure you need.

These questions can help you identify some frameworks to try:

In the examples of manifestos you have seen so far, what frameworks or structures appealed to you? Why?

Take a look at your collection of statements. Does the material itself suggest a particular type of framework that interests you?

If patterns emerged when you were exploring the material you collected, is there a framework in there you might want to try?

Choose a few appealing frameworks to try. One round at a time, rearrange your statements, using a framework to give your statements some deliberate relationships. Each type of framework should help you to prioritize or coordinate your statements in a different way. After each round, take a few minutes to reflect on these questions:

Does this framework help me figure out why these statements resonate with me?

Does it help me connect them with my values or communicate my identity or ethics?

Take time to review and rework your content based on your answers.

FORM & STYLE CREATE MEANING. THEY SHOULD MATTER TO YOU.

The Medium Is the Message

Picture, in your mind's eye, the word *love*. Now picture it as a mural on a giant wall. Now see a T-shirt with the word *love* on it, and then a tattoo of the word *love,* a teddy bear with the word *love* on it, and finally, a television advertisement with the word *love* in it. The methods and formats that we use to carry messages change the meaning of the message itself.

The communication theorist Marshall McLuhan is famous for his saying "the medium is the message." He pointed out how the various technologies that transmit our messages change us in ways that are profound. It's worth considering this idea in a little more depth to help you determine what kind of medium will be right for your manifesto.

The way a message reaches us changes the way we think about it. Before printing presses became more widely adopted, reading and writing were the province of a small group of learned people involved in religious practice, commerce, or governance. For most people, becoming a reader or writer wasn't possible, useful, or necessary. The printed word changed that, and then it changed everything else: our methods of self-expression, the ways we communicate with one another, our societal relationships, our language, our communities, and our world. And every medium for communication does the same thing. Think about how we've changed our messages to adapt to texting or Twitter. McLuhan's idea expressed how "we shape our tools and thereafter our tools shape us," molding us with their capabilities and determining our behaviors. This might not be all that surprising anymore, but it's still hard to hear that we are all less in control of our output than we might think we are.

As McLuhan pointed out, it's not just the content of the message that matters; it's also where and when you see it or hear it and how it is presented that determine its meaning to you: the color, size, and shape of type in a printed message; how loud and the kind of voice and tone in an audio message; what's on next to your video, or before and after it, as well as what you did right before seeing it, and what you are about to do after. It's the context in which you see something.

Artists and designers love the connections and meanings that can be made between messages by the medium itself. The relationships between messages can make each of them more powerful, emotional, and memorable. You can use these qualities to your advantage to choose **a medium for your manifesto that will deliver what you need, when and where you need it, and that will shape your own behavior in the way you want.**

Find Your Format

How you say it is just as important as what you say. Each format changes the meaning of your words and creates a different type of communication experience or moment. Maybe you need a moment to listen to yourself. You might want to communicate clearly to others or to make a decision or get some perspective. Whatever the experience is that you need from your manifesto, there's a medium that can help you achieve it. Like the frameworks that you've been playing with, some formats are very targeted, assertive, and structured in the type of communication experience that they create—like a billboard on the side of the highway, shouting about what you should buy—and others are more open-ended, flexible, and subtle.

The first format you're going to work with is a collage. It's a great way to prototype a manifesto because it takes so little effort to get started. A collage is an almost endlessly flexible medium. You can bring a huge variety of frameworks into it, and even mock up other media with it. It doesn't require preparation or equipment beyond scissors and a glue stick. Right now you can experiment without a lot of emotional investment or risk.

Find yourself a base to work on. I prefer to use an 11 by 17-inch piece of heavy paper or cardboard. You could buy something similar at a craft store or office supply place, but you probably already have something in your recycling

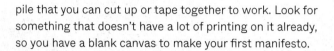

pile that you can cut up or tape together to work. Look for something that doesn't have a lot of printing on it already, so you have a blank canvas to make your first manifesto.

Give yourself thirty minutes to take your clippings and arrange them on your canvas in a way that is meaningful to you. You've done quite a bit of work already, interrogating and interpreting your choices, digging for insights, and exploring frameworks. You may already have a layout in mind that uses one of the frameworks you've tried. But if you don't, try not to get too hung up on it. Trust that you know what you like, and treat this step as another opportunity to ask yourself what you feel, think, and believe.

As you work, you can use colored markers, tape, or any other craft or art supplies you have on hand to emphasize, embellish, amend, or add to your manifesto. If you need to make new statements, you can cut out the letters or words that you need from your scraps, or type them and print them out, or just write them in freehand. This does not have to be museum-quality artwork. It's a prototype. But don't treat it like a throwaway either. You should be striving to make something that you want to hang on to. Treat it with respect.

At the end of thirty minutes (or whenever you feel you've done enough), stand back and take a look at your work. It might look a little like a Frankenstein-inspired ransom note, but it should also be an authentic representation of the things you believe in and aspire to.

Congratulations! You've got your first manifesto. Now what?

The next step is to do a little testing with your new prototype. But before we go there, a word more about formats and how they will figure into future versions of your manifesto.

While I can pretty much guarantee that a collage will work for your first prototype, ultimately it might not be the format that works best for your manifesto. You might need something with more gravitas or something more intimate. You might want to go digital or move from a visual medium to audio or video. There are so many to choose from. A propaganda poster or a bumper sticker? A mural or a needlework sampler? Tattooed or typed?

Here are some questions to help you think about formats as you continue to work your work:

> **When do you need to be reminded of your manifesto? First thing in the morning? Last thing at night? Right before a meeting? When you feel frustrated?**
>
> **What will be accessible to you at that moment? Is it the background on your phone, the sticky note on your bathroom mirror, an automated email you get every day? A laminated card you put in your wallet?**
>
> **How much detail do you need? Just the headlines? Or do you need to go deeper?**

How will you share it? With people close to you? Your family or your team? Publicly?

As you test and revise the content of your manifesto, you should also be looking for the right medium for your message.

Trust It and Test It

At this point, it's good to remember that a manifesto is a document for right now. Today's manifesto is your truth for today. Next week or next year you could (and probably should) make a new manifesto. The power of a manifesto is its immediacy and presence, but it is useful only as long as it is relevant. Like a strong scientific hypothesis, it is a statement that is constantly testing for the truth.

Make your manifesto a living document. For this, you need to adopt a learning mindset. When you find new truths, take time to look closely at the old ones. Grow and change and learn. Let your manifesto be a tool to help you get better and wiser. Practice both trusting and testing your manifesto—giving it an opportunity to teach you about yourself, your work, and the way those two things fit together.

A personal manifesto can help you synthesize new ideas and incorporate learning into your life. Be brave enough to take action when it counts. Develop the grit to keep after your goals. Inform your intuition. Keep your balance as you change to meet the moment. Make decisions that make sense and are true to yourself and respectful to others. Finally, none of those principles and practices can be effective without a practice of reflection so that you can learn your way into the future.

You've already spent time and energy getting your thoughts, feelings, and beliefs out of your head and onto the page in front of you. Let me now push you to get it even further out there. Trust that your manifesto is an authentic expression, but also trust that it isn't perfect or even finished. And trust in other people to help you get it there. In the same way that you can push and amplify your thinking and understanding by using physical materials and visual relationships outside of yourself, you can also challenge and strengthen them with the presence of another person's thinking.

In the following exercise, you'll try to explain what you mean to another person by showing them your manifesto and walking them through your statements, frameworks, and ideas. You may fail to get them to understand everything, but you may also express some things that are even closer to the root of your own beliefs, in your own words. When other people have a chance to misunderstand, ask questions, and discuss with you, it can open up a new way of considering your work or provide the inkling of a new idea. No matter what comes of this exercise, it will extend your ability to think.

Reflect and Renew

When you've made something on your own that feels personal, it can be hard to let someone else in on it. And it can feel especially risky to show an early prototype—something as low-resolution as your first Franken-manifesto—to someone who has no idea about what you're up to. Here are a few ways to bolster your own thinking and to engage people to help you. Each interaction will produce different results. All of them are useful to do—and to do more than once.

Talk to yourself

Test and critique your own work. Put your manifesto somewhere you'll see it frequently. This might be near a desk you often use, on your bathroom mirror, or as the background for your phone. Now go about living your life. Every time you encounter it, think about what you've been up to and ask yourself:

Does anything I'm reading in my manifesto relate to what I've been doing or am about to do?

Based on this, would I change anything about what I've done or am about to do? How?

What else should I be thinking about or remembering right now that I could include?

When and where would be the best place for me to see or hear this?

Partner up

Find a kindred spirit—a friend or a colleague who is interested in doing this work at the same time as you are. Go through the exercises alongside one another and take time to share your experiences. When you have both produced your first manifesto, get together to share and debrief your work.

Take a few minutes to look at each other's work, and take turns walking each other through your manifestos.

Ask each other questions provoked by what you've seen and heard. Why did they choose this statement or that framework? What does it mean to them?

Give each other the opportunity to explain deeper reasonings and ideas.

When you are the listener, take notes, and then reflect what you heard to your partner.

Ask your partner to look at your manifesto carefully and describe to you, as fully as they can, another person (not you) who might have written it.

> Who could that person be? What do they care about? What kind of work might they do? Why did they make this manifesto? Where do they keep it, show it, or use it?

Choose a mentor

Is there a person in your life who knows you fairly well, someone you trust and admire, who might be receptive to giving you feedback on your manifesto? Talk to them.

Tell them about what you are doing and give them some background on the exercise.

Before you start your work, you might want to have a preliminary, general conversation about values, beliefs, and ethics to get some perspective from them.

Ask them directly if they would be willing to give you some feedback on your manifesto to help improve your self-awareness and do the best work you can.

When you show your mentor your prototype manifesto, ask them:

> What do you think I am trying to communicate?

What does it reveal about me that you didn't know about me? How?

What else do you know about me or see in me that doesn't seem to be included?

Go wide

If you've been picking up what I've been laying down, you might realize that your first manifesto actually is not as precious as you might think. Especially if your eventual goal is for your manifesto to be public, the more you get it out there and talk about it, the sooner you'll learn about it. Here are a few ideas for you to get feedback from a bigger pool of folks, if you're comfortable with that:

Use your manifesto as your background for video calls. Each call becomes an opportunity to have a quick chat with someone about your manifesto and get some casual feedback or ideas from others.

Post it on a social media channel that you trust. While I don't recommend letting internet trolls have at your manifesto, if there is a closed, private group or other digital community that you trust, consider sharing it there. Give it a little context and see what kinds of questions people ask.

No particular methodology for promoting self-awareness or building a moral landscape is the right one for every person, context, or moment. What would be the point of creating any tool for growth and change that depends on learning from others, if the tool itself can't change in the hands of others? **This manifesto project is open source.** My hope is that you will use it and adapt it in ways that will promote the search for values in your work, no matter what kind of work it is. In the next chapter, you'll see a few examples of the ways in which my fellow designers and educators at the d.school have adapted the manifesto project for their own needs. I hope they'll inspire you to do the same.

HOLD MY HAND

PRIOR

IMPOSSIBLE TO BE HERE ALONE

ASK FOR HELP

PRIOR NURSE

LET ME

IT'S
HEAL
ING

LET'S READ TOGETHER

TELL YOUR STORY

LET ME HOLD YOU CLOSE

BE READY TO HELP

YOUR WOUND

Rick Griffith

CULTIVATE

5

LOOK HARDER

FIND THE LOVE

LOOK AROUND YOU

IT'S

SING YOUR SONG

BE BOLD

Go Open Source

In 1973 Dolly Parton wrote the song "I Will Always Love You" as a sweet farewell to her long-time musical partner, Porter Wagoner. It was a hit with her fans. But in 1992, Whitney Houston recorded a power ballad cover of "I Will Always Love You" for the film *The Bodyguard* that brought the house down and blew the roof off the Billboard charts. In an interview with Oprah Winfrey, Dolly related that when she heard Whitney's rendition for the first time, on the radio in her car, "My heart just started to beat so fast and it was the most overwhelming thing. I was shot so full of adrenaline and energy, I had to pull off the road because I was afraid that I would wreck. I pulled over quick as I could to listen to that whole song. I could not believe how she did that. I mean, how beautiful it was that my little song had turned into that." Like Aretha Franklin singing Otis Redding's "Respect," Whitney Houston pushed the power and meaning of Dolly Parton's song beyond where she might ever have thought it could go. This is what our work can do when we release it into the hands of others, and what their work can sometimes do in our own hands.

This manifesto project can work in the same way. Your own personal manifesto is a groundbreaking and essential guide, but when you open up to making a manifesto with a group or share it with others, it can reach a whole new level of impact and meaning. My colleagues at the d.school have adapted the manifesto project for their own classes, workshops, and personal use, and the examples in this chapter come from their work. With them, you can use the manifesto project to deepen your personal and collective learning, explore and experiment with identity, build trust and community, create transparency, and set the ground rules for a collective culture. Take your manifesto momentum and turn it into a bridge to your community—a collectively built contract that serves as a catalyst for change.

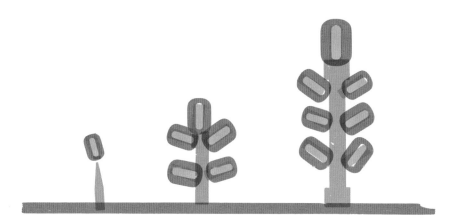

Synthesize Your Learning

For a long time, the most asked question at the end of every professional workshop at the d.school was something like, "This design s*** is amazing! But how do I bring it home?" This is not an idle question. Students in the d.school's executive education program have plenty of experience leading and working with teams in professional contexts, from small nonprofits to huge Fortune 500 companies. They know that retaining and using new knowledge is different from and often more difficult than acquiring it. They were really asking "How do I hang on to all these new ideas and behaviors I've learned in a company where no one else knows about them and they are more than likely going to get trampled in the next deadline rush?"

Deep learning is not only about the acquisition of fascinating new bits and bobs of information. In its most holistic form, it is the integration of new experiences (including all those cool factoids) into your conceptualization of the world in a way that enables you to act and react differently than you've been able to before. Synthesizing new experiences and knowledge into new beliefs and actions can happen only if you take time to reflect on the new stuff and actually process it into the old.

These days the d.school's executive education team—Jeremy Utley, Perry Klebahn, and Dr. Kathryn Segovia—focus a significant part of their time on the tools that "take it home" from workshops packed with a huge variety of topics and modes of learning. Participants experience hands-on exercises in leadership skills, lectures on the emotional nature of decision making, practicums on risk taking that leave participants weak in the knees, and team-based innovation projects that demonstrate the power and perils of collaboration. Sounds like your basic week of working, living, managing, or parenting, right?

Everyone is trying to incorporate new knowledge into the working models of their world all the time. Integrating these types of diverse experiences is not exactly easy. But the process can be pretty straightforward. To do it, our team puts new knowledge next to old and asks the honest question "What actually matters to you?"

Try this variation when you have a significant learning experience (it could be in a class, a major project, or a meaningful personal experience) and you want to be intentional about bringing the value of that experience into your daily life or to hang onto the ideas long enough for them to have a chance to change how you behave.

Ask yourself some serious questions

Reflect on your learning and deliberately question whether anything you have experienced has changed the way you want to act or react in the future.

What has changed about what you believe or value?

What new behaviors do you want to practice?

What new ideas do you want to champion?

Make yourself a cheat sheet

Side by side with the manifestos in your pack, add an extra page or two of significant notes from your own experience—things you've learned and want to hold onto. Put them together with the quick-start pack of manifestos we've suggested or any other group of manifestos you're excited to use.

Now integrate!

Go through the basic steps of the manifesto project. As you are collecting statements for your manifesto, take your time going through your extra notes. Choose the statements that represent the learning you feel most passionate about and the new behaviors you want to commit to, and incorporate them into your manifesto.

By placing your new ideas and experiences side by side with inspirational manifestos that touch on deeply held values and beliefs, you are actively comparing your newest learning with your existing attitudes and values and making deliberate choices to incorporate what you feel is most useful to you and your work.

Be Authentic with Others

When you are doing work that is hard, that encounters failure, resistance, and setbacks, your values and goals can provide you with feelings of support. If values and goals are held collectively, those supportive feelings can be amplified. But if expressing feelings, beliefs, and values is considered "too much" in your workplace or community, you won't have access to that kind of support. A manifesto can help turn that around.

Jess Brown and Louie Montoya teach and research at the d.school about the intersection of racial equity and design. They help people who are doing the hard work of standing up for social justice to support themselves and their communities. Their version of the manifesto project is a direct engagement with your sense of identity and purpose and a method for groups of committed people to connect authentically with each other. They want you to take your stance and stand behind what you believe in a shareable way. Their project sets aside time for you to recruit yourself to this work, get clarity on your *why,* and improve your ability to communicate that *why* with others. As their friend Courtlandt Butts says, "Your *why* has to be stronger than your *why not.*" If your *why* is not stronger, you won't continue through tension and roadblocks.

THE THINGS YOU LEARN CAN CHANGE YOU IF YOU LET THEM.

In the beginning, share

As part of their riff on the manifesto project, Louie and Jess ask every person to share a piece of text, no more than a few pages, that has inspired or motivated them. It could be any poem, essay, rousing speech, quote, or mission statement that has had an impact on how they work, live, and resist oppressive systems. This gives each person an opportunity to bring inspiration to the community and to see how that gift is received.

Share in the middle

Behind the scenes, everyone's texts are compiled and added to the source material for the manifesto project pack that has been made for everyone. Each person in the group does the manifesto project individually, and when they come back together to look at each other's manifestos, Jess loves the moment when "folks light up as they see evidence of the inspiration they submitted on another person's manifesto."

Share at last

After everyone has made their own manifestos, Jess and Louie have everyone come together and share them with each other. Individuals develop trust and a sense of community when they share their beliefs with a larger group. When exploring manifestos in this way, it's important to talk about each one, hear from the maker, ask questions, and have conversations about points that come up. This develops relationships and sets a group dynamic based on shared experiences and conversations. It highlights every individual and allows people to feel truly seen.

For Louie and Jess and the people they work with, the manifesto project is a moment to share with integrity, to inspire one another, building community and setting a supportive foundation for serious and significant work.

Cultivate

Experiment with Yourself

Do you feel stuck? How long has it been since you considered whether the identity you have created for yourself is really the one you want? Are you open to the possibility of change? When you encounter new ideas and methods that challenge your ways of thinking, are you willing to consider revising your values and goals? To experiment with new methods and see yourself in new ways? To hold your mind open a little bit rather than going for closure right away? This is the sweet spot for your mindset when you take on the manifesto project—willing to be actively experimental, ready for self-discovery.

My colleague Leticia Britos Cavagnaro says, "The most impactful aspect of learning is its power to transform who we are. Reflection provides the mirror to look at our identities and their evolution through the process of *learning to become,* rather than *learning about.*" An inveterate experimenter with a PhD in developmental biology, Leticia is constantly asking questions at the d.school about how learning works, how design works, and how they can work together better. She sees reflection as one of the most powerful conduits for learning and change, as a way to both promote growth and prevent yourself from getting stuck.

In Leticia's hands, the manifesto project is an invitation to reflect, to experiment with your identity and expand your capacity for self-awareness. Her variation is designed for the times when you have encountered new and different ways of working and being and are thinking, *What does this mean for me and my goals? How do I want to work moving forward? What kind of person do I want to be?* Her exercise is a series of experimental variations on the manifesto project, a guide to creating multiple perspectives on your learning, your identity, and the impact that you want to make in the world.

Experiment with direction

Create a manifesto that is about your identity.

Create a manifesto about the impact that you want to make in the world.

Create a manifesto that is about who you are right now.

Create a manifesto that is about who you want to be in the future.

Experiment with rhythm and timing

Create a manifesto today and another one tomorrow.

Create one manifesto a day for a week.

Experiment with input

Start with twenty manifestos as your inspiration.

Find a random document on your computer. Print one page and use it as your inspiration.

Create a manifesto from a blank page.

Experiment with output

Create a one-phrase or one-sentence manifesto.

Write it with a stick in the sand or the dirt.

Now carve it into wood or chisel it into stone.
Or paint it on canvas or print it large.

Experiment with the audience

Create a manifesto exclusively for yourself, one that no one else will see.

Create a manifesto that is public, available to everyone.

Ask questions about your manifestos

What differences do you notice between your manifestos? What do they have in common?

Did you surprise yourself or contradict yourself?

Did you learn that you value something that you didn't know you valued?

In your manifestos, where are you using your gut and where are you more analytical?

Where do you want each of your manifestos to show up for you? Or when? Or how?

What do your answers to each of these questions suggest to you about your goals, values, ethics, or biases?

Each variation of your manifesto and every question you ask is an opportunity to understand and communicate another facet of your whole self. Each one is a moment of possibility—to lean into new behaviors, to question your motives, and to expand your identity. It might feel like reflection, but introspection of this kind is actually forward looking. Leticia calls it "proflection" rather than reflection. This is how you grow and keep growing.

Collaborate with Trust

Humans are social beings. To achieve truly great things, we need to come together. When we articulate our common values and goals, it's easier and more effective to do the things we set out to do together. Creating a collective manifesto can be a great tool for a group to communicate and negotiate its way into authentic collaboration. What happens if your team can't meet in person—say, because there's a global pandemic with stay-at-home orders in place?

Manasa Yeturu began planning to incorporate the manifesto project into her lesson plans for Design for Extreme Affordability as soon as she arrived at the d.school in the autumn of 2019. Extreme, as it's called, is one of the d.school's flagship classes that focuses on social impact projects that connect teams of students based at Stanford with people in organizations all over the world. Her role on the team includes teaching about ethics, positionality, and bias, and she pushes her students to continually reflect on how they want to show up in their work both individually and as a team. As the COVID-19 pandemic gripped the world through 2020 and 2021, the Extreme teams were unable to connect in person with their teams or their project partners. Yet Manasa managed to help them create collective norms and collaborative goals using her take on the manifesto project, which is a series of concentric rings, focused first on an individual, then a team, then a community.

Center ring: your own manifesto

Each group member makes their own individual manifesto first. The group shares their manifestos with each other. You can do this in person or online. Make time to speak with each other as a group. Give each person in your group the opportunity to introduce their manifesto and provide time for the whole group to reflect on the process.

Middle ring: the group's manifesto

Ask everyone to offer a piece of text that represents a core value to the group. It could be from their own manifesto or from elsewhere. Take time as a group to discuss these and identify the kinds of values they represent. If your group is small, do the work to synthesize your contributions collectively. If it's a large group, nominate some leadership to take the first pass at creating a synthesized manifesto, and then discuss it and revise it as a group. In Manasa's class, each small group does this together, and then they do it as a whole class.

Outer ring: a social contract with your project partners

Does your group work in collaboration with or in service of other people or organizations? Manasa's student teams work with both local and international organizations who have goals and values of their own. The teams invite their partner organizations to share their goals and values, and together they create a manifesto for the project and a social contract to guide their work.

In this exercise, by beginning with each individual and moving toward progressively larger groupings, collective values emerge from individual goals, respect is given to each person, and trust is built in the group. When groups come together, they have a common method to build transparency and trust into their working relationships.

Manifesto making as a group requires the same level of integrity and introspection as individual work. It's not about one person setting the agenda and having others sign on. It's not a bunch of drivel that's all talk and no action, or a manifesto that applies only to some people in the group. And it's definitely not dogma, which can entrap people into actions that are irrelevant or harmful. A great group manifesto allows separate people to come together to form collective goals and common ethics. This kind of group lives and learns just as much as any individual.

The people you learn with and work with and live with can change you, too—and you should let them. Your life and work are enriched by interacting with other people. One of the best reasons to know yourself better is so that you can connect better with others.

YOU CAN POSSIBLY UNDERSTAND

EVERYTHING IS MORE COMPLICATED THAN

Coda

In my own personal manifesto, there is one statement that underlies everything else: "Everything is more complicated that you can possibly understand."

I came to this knowledge through experiences that were diversely painful, beautiful, confusing, crushing, and cathartic. In other words, by living. This mantra is my reminder to constantly reach for humility, to extend the benefit of the doubt, to exercise compassion, and to be cautious of both my own assessments of any situation and the assertions of others. It is a poem to the beauty and mystery of complexity, and to the frustration of never knowing enough. It's good for moments of defeat. It props me up by reminding me that screwing up is totally normal. And it's good for the high points too, where it tempers my sweet victories with a strong dash of realism. It points out that my goals are helplessly tied up with the goals of others, and that my values are truly known only to me. I use it nearly every day.

In my mind's eye, the life I'm navigating looks like an ocean, incredibly vast and in constant motion. At any given moment the pieces of my manifesto, like the one just offered, help make up the boat I'm in. But manifestos don't sail themselves. They'll keep you upright and balanced in the waves only as long as you're paying attention, managing your sails, adjusting your heading, and bailing out the hull. You've got to keep working on them to keep moving forward.

Making a manifesto is a practice of self-awareness, but it's not just for you. By knowing yourself better, you can do better work with others. And your manifesto may be your boat, but it's not the only way to travel. **In the end, if you abandon ship on your manifesto but hold fast to your values, your beliefs, and your self-awareness, we'll all make it safely to shore.**

I LIKE QUIET EVEN THOUGH I'M LOUD.

RICK GRIFFITH: Master Manifester

Rick Griffith is a graphic designer and master letterpress printer. His work is an exploration of language, history, politics, science, music, and ethics—typographically-focused and relevant. He is known as a passionate advocate for design.

Rick was born and raised in Southeast London and immigrated to the U.S. in the late 1980s. His early jobs at Washington DC record stores turned him on to graphic design. A (short) freelance career on Madison Avenue funded his first practice, RGD (Rick Griffith Design), and his love of design (and his partner Debra Johnson) sustains the design practice, MATTER, which, over the last two decades, has grown into an ambidextrous design consultancy, print shop, workshop, and retail bookstore.

From his home in Denver or his creative atelier in Brooklyn, Rick travels the world as a visiting artist, lecturer, and educator—sharing his enthusiasm and knowledge with the next generation of designers—and contributing critical dialogue regarding graphic design as a broad discipline in the service of community and industry.

Rick's true orientation is toward self-reliance, disruption, creative compassion, and independent thought.

For most of us, life is long—for a lot of reasons, we might begin to act like it.

If we are going to love design, make design useful, give design power and authority, and focus on its service to others—well, we are also going to have to know more. Firstly, know ourselves more. Know our planet more. Know our price more. Know more geography, know more physics, know more about loss and grief, know more about love and joy. Not just care about—but know more about—the impact of our actions on others. . . .

Design, like many constructs, is a human invention full of human action. We have to be willing to do it for each other—if we do this work at all. . . .

I LOVE DESIGN SO MUCH. I BELIEVE GOOD DESIGN SHOULD HAVE NO VICTIMS.

—from "A Love Letter to Design, a List of Demands, and a Stern Look," by Rick Griffith

Acknowledgments

First of all, I would like to thank *you*—thank you for
wanting to live in and work with your values. You, and all
the others who are doing the same thing, whether with a
manifesto or without, are who keep me getting up in the
morning. I am grateful to my parents and my family who
gave me my foundational beliefs, to my friends and my
communities who built and shaped my values with me,
and to my husband and children who show me how to
try and live them every day.

To my many colleagues and collaborators at the d.school,
your voices resound in this book. Thank you for sharing and
shaping my work with me over the past fifteen years. I owe
much to Julian Gorodsky, who first helped me to assign a
problem to its rightful owner and stay in discomfort long
enough for it to teach me something. And I want to thank
both Michael Hawley and George Kembel, who hired me
at MIT and Stanford respectively, and who believed in me
before I knew what I believed.

In this work particularly, I would like to thank Scott Doorley
for believing in us all, and in me especially. I am so grateful
for the extraordinary generosity of your time, talent, and
vision in the service of this effort. To my editor Jenn Brown,
this work and all our work is made so much better by your
shaping and stitching. Your gentle hand produces strength
and structure. To the incredible editorial, design, and

production team at Ten Speed Press, thank you for helping us to bring our wild ideas to fruition with such expertise and elegance. And a particular thanks to Annie Marino, for the extraordinary effort of design and illustration that bring such joy and life to this little book.

And finally, with gratitude to Rick Griffith, for trusting us with your work. It is an honor beyond measure, which I will endeavor to deserve.

Sources

For links to, and list of, the resources mentioned in this book—and to add to the library of manifestos—visit **d.school.stanford.edu/books/manifestos**.

Index

Published in the United States by Ten Speed Press, an imprint of
Random House, a division of Penguin Random House LLC, New York.
TenSpeed.com
RandomHouseBooks.com

Ten Speed Press and the Ten Speed Press colophon are registered trademarks
of Penguin Random House LLC.

Images in the third manifesto are in the public domain and from the Smithsonian
Archive from top to bottom: Black and white poster of Huey Newton and Bobby Seale,
ca. 1971. Collection of the Smithsonian National Museum of African American History
and Culture. John Roy Lynch, c. 1882. National Portrait Gallery, Smithsonian Institution.
Jackie Robinson, 1949. National Portrait Gallery, Smithsonian Institution. Ida B. Wells,
c. 1893. National Portrait Gallery, Smithsonian Institution.

Typefaces: Hope Meng's d.sign, Dinamo's Whyte, and Delta Bravo's Clariday Slab

Library of Congress Cataloging-in-Publication Data
Names: Burgess-Auburn, Charlotte, author. | Griffith, Rick, illustrator. |
   Hasso Plattner Institute of Design (Stanford University), issuing body.
Title: You need a manifesto : how to craft your convictions and put them to
   work / Charlotte Burgess Auburn ; manifestos and art by Rick Griffith.
Description: First edition. | California : Ten Speed Press, [2022] |
   Includes bibliographical references and index.
Identifiers: LCCN 2021052355 (print) | LCCN 2021052356 (ebook) |
   ISBN 9781984858061 (trade paperback) | ISBN 9781984858078 (ebook)
Subjects: LCSH: Self-actualization (Psychology) | Self-realization. |
   Intention. | Creative ability. | Goal (Psychology)
Classification: LCC BF637.S4 B868 2022 (print) | LCC BF637.S4 (ebook) |
   DDC 155.2—dc23/eng/20220322
LC record available at https://lccn.loc.gov/2021052355
LC ebook record available at https://lccn.loc.gov/2021052356

Trade Paperback ISBN: 978-1-9848-5806-1
eBook ISBN: 978-1-9848-5807-8

Printed in China

Illustrations by Annie Marino
Acquiring editor: Hannah Rahill | Editor: Kim Keller
Designer: Annie Marino | Art director: Emma Campion
Production designer: Mari Gill
Production and prepress color manager: Jane Chinn
Copyeditor: Kristi Hein | Proofreader: Lisa Brousseau | Indexer: Andrew Lopez
Publicist: David Hawk | Marketer: Windy Dorresteyn
Stanford d.school creative team: Scott Doorley and Jennifer Brown

10 9 8 7 6 5 4 3 2 1

First Edition